LOST CHRONICLES OF LIGHT

Book 1 - A Christian Fantasy Adventure

Abbie Rose

Staten House

LOST CHRONICLES OF LIGHT

Editing & Layout by Abiegail Rose

Book Cover by Abiegail Rose

Contents

1

The Secret in the Woods

Naomi Williams stood on the edge of the forest, squinting against the bright summer sun. Her heart raced with excitement, a familiar feeling that always surfaced when she was about to dive into something unknown. The towering trees ahead were thick with shadows, and somewhere within those shadows lay the ruins—the place she'd been talking about for weeks. Her fingers toyed with the strap of her backpack, the weight of the flashlight inside reminding her of her careful planning.

"I don't see what the big deal is." Luke Miller's voice cut through the air, his hands shoved deep into his cargo pants pockets. He glanced at her with a raised eyebrow, the usual skepticism clear in his pale blue eyes. "It's just some old chapel or something. You've been going on about it all week."

Naomi rolled her eyes but couldn't suppress a smile. Luke always acted like he wasn't interested in her ideas, but somehow, he was always right by her side when things got interesting.

"Just wait," she said, her eyes gleaming. "I have a feeling about this place."

"A feeling," Luke repeated, smirking. "Like one of those 'gut feelings'? The ones where you're almost always right?"

"Exactly," she replied, adjusting her glasses and starting toward the narrow path that wound into the woods. "You'll see."

The forest around them buzzed with life. Birds chirped overhead, and the scent of pine filled the air. Naomi inhaled deeply, savoring the smell. There was something about the woods that made her feel alive—like anything could happen. Behind her, Luke trudged along, kicking at stones with each step. She knew he wasn't big on faith, or mystery for that matter, but there was no denying he loved a good adventure. That's why he was there, even if he wouldn't admit it.

The two friends had been inseparable since kindergarten. They balanced each other out—Naomi, the dreamer, always chasing after something bigger, and Luke, the realist, the one who questioned everything. It worked, even when they bickered.

After what felt like forever, the trees parted, revealing the ruins she had been so eager to find. It was smaller than she expected, just a crumbling stone chapel that looked like it had been swallowed by the forest years ago. Vines twisted around the broken pillars, and moss clung to the stone like a second skin. Sunlight filtered through the gaps in the canopy, casting long, eerie shadows on the ground.

"Whoa," Luke muttered, his skepticism fading as he stepped closer to the ruins. "Okay, maybe this is a little cool."

Naomi grinned, feeling a swell of satisfaction. "Told you."

Together, they approached the chapel, the atmosphere around them growing heavy, like the forest itself was holding its breath. The stones underfoot were cool and damp, and the air seemed to grow thicker as they neared the entrance—a gaping hole where the door had once stood.

Naomi's pulse quickened. This was it. This was what she had been waiting for.

"Careful," Luke said, his voice lower now, more serious. "This place looks like it's ready to fall apart."

"Relax," Naomi whispered, stepping inside. "I've got this."

Inside, the chapel was even smaller. Most of the roof had caved in, and fallen beams lay scattered across the floor, but there was something about the place that made Naomi feel like it was more than just an old ruin. Dust floated in the shafts of light that spilled through the cracks above, and the smell of damp stone filled the air.

Naomi wandered further in, her fingers brushing against the stone walls. There was something here, she could feel it. Something hidden beneath the layers of time. She scanned the room, her eyes lingering on a large stone near the far wall.

"That rock looks weird," Luke pointed out, following her gaze. "Like, out of place."

Naomi nodded, her heart pounding in her chest. "Help me move it."

Luke groaned, but he didn't argue. Together, they shoved the heavy stone aside, revealing a narrow hole beneath it. Naomi's breath caught in her throat as she peered into the darkness.

"There's something down there," she said, barely above a whisper.

Luke leaned over, squinting into the hole. "I don't see anything."

Naomi reached into her backpack, pulling out the flashlight she'd packed. With a flick, the beam of light cut through the shadows, revealing a small, dusty chamber beneath the floor.

"There," Naomi said, pointing.

At the bottom of the hole, half-buried in dirt, was an old book, its leather cover cracked and worn. But what made Naomi's heart stop was the faint glow emanating from its edges, as if the book itself was alive.

Luke stared, wide-eyed. "What is that?"

Naomi didn't answer. She dropped to her knees, reaching down into the hole. The moment her fingers touched the book's surface, warmth shot through her hand, spreading up her arm like fire.

"Naomi, wait—" Luke started, but it was too late.

As Naomi pulled the book free, a rush of wind swept through the chapel, stirring the dust and leaves around them. The temperature dropped, and the light from the book grew brighter, pulsing with a rhythm like a heartbeat.

Naomi's breath hitched. This was no ordinary book.

Luke backed up, his eyes wide with a mix of awe and fear. "What...what did you just do?"

Naomi stood slowly, cradling the glowing book in her hands. She had no idea what she had done, but there was one thing she knew for sure.

Their lives were about to change forever.

2

THE BOOK OF LIGHT

NAOMI STOOD FROZEN, THE glow of the ancient book radiating from her hands. It was unlike anything she had ever felt—warm, but not in a way that could be explained by temperature alone. It was as if the light itself was alive, pulsing gently against her fingertips, drawing her closer to something she couldn't yet name.

Luke took a hesitant step back, his wide eyes darting between Naomi and the book. "Seriously, Naomi, what is that thing?"

She didn't answer immediately. Her eyes were locked on the swirling gold lines and symbols that covered the leather-bound cover. They shifted ever so slightly, almost as if they were breathing. Naomi's mind raced, trying to connect the dots, but nothing made sense. It was like all the rules of the world had been tossed out the window.

"I...I don't know," she finally whispered. "But I think it's something we're supposed to find."

Luke gave her a skeptical look, crossing his arms. "Supposed to find? Since when do books glow? You think this thing's some kind of magic?"

Naomi bit her lip, her heart thudding in her chest. It sounded crazy when Luke said it out loud, but then again, nothing about this moment was normal. She crouched down, placing the book on the cracked stone floor of the chapel, its glow casting long shadows on the crumbling walls around them. The light flickered, almost as if it was waiting for something.

"There's only one way to find out," Naomi said, her voice steadier than she felt.

Luke sighed, running a hand through his messy hair. "I knew I shouldn't have followed you into this creepy place."

Naomi grinned at him, the tension between them easing just a little. "But you did."

Before he could respond, the book gave a sudden shudder, and the glowing lines on its surface began to move faster, swirling and twisting in intricate patterns. Naomi gasped, her hand hovering above the cover but not touching it. It was as if the book was alive, reacting to their presence.

"What's happening?" Luke asked, his voice lower now, more cautious.

"I don't know," Naomi admitted. She leaned closer, her breath catching in her throat. The light intensified, and then, with a soft click, the cover of the book slowly lifted open.

The pages inside were ancient, yellowed with age, and covered in what looked like handwritten text—except it wasn't any language Naomi had ever seen before. Strange symbols filled the pages, glowing faintly in the same golden light that had surrounded the book. But as Naomi looked closer, she realized something else.

The pages weren't all filled. In fact, many of them were blank.

"Why are some of the pages empty?" Luke asked, stepping closer now, his earlier hesitation melting away.

"I don't know," Naomi said, her fingers lightly brushing one of the blank pages. As soon as her hand made contact, a sharp tingling sensation shot up her arm, and she pulled back with a gasp.

"What happened?" Luke's voice was tight with concern.

Naomi shook her head, flexing her fingers. "I don't know, but...it feels like this book is waiting for something. Like it's waiting for us."

"Us?" Luke repeated, his voice thick with disbelief. "Why would it be waiting for us?"

Naomi wasn't sure, but deep down, she felt it—the same feeling she had when they'd first stumbled upon the ruins, the feeling that something was calling to her, to them. Her eyes fell on the symbols that glowed faintly on the filled pages, her mind racing. She knew what she had to do.

"We need to read it," she said, her voice more confident now.

"Read it?" Luke looked at her like she was crazy. "Naomi, we can't even understand this language! How are we supposed to—"

But as Naomi stared at the symbols, something incredible happened. The glowing lines on the page began to shift again, slowly rearranging them-selves into words that she could understand. The strange symbols transformed, letter by letter, until they formed sentences, clear and perfect in English.

"It's changing," Naomi whispered, her eyes wide.

Luke leaned over her shoulder, his face a mix of awe and confusion. "What the..."

Naomi's fingers traced the first line of text, the words shimmering softly in the dim light of the chapel.

A gasp escaped her lips. The pages were blank. At least, they were supposed to be.

"Look at this," Naomi whispered, her voice trem-bling with awe as she turned the first page.

Letters began to appear, as if an invisible hand were writing before their eyes. The ink glowed faintly, forming words in a language Naomi didn't recognize. The script was elegant, ancient-looking, and as the words unfurled across the page, Naomi felt something stir deep inside her, something both familiar and unknown.

Luke leaned in, his breath shallow as he tried to make sense of what was happening. "What does it say?"

"I—I don't know," Naomi stammered, her eyes glued to the glowing letters. "But...I think I can read it."

Luke shot her a look of disbelief. "How? You've never seen that language before."

Naomi shook her head, biting her lip. "I don't know. I just... I feel like I can understand it."

She squinted, focusing on the swirling script, and as she did, the words seemed to shift, transforming into something more familiar. She could almost hear a soft whisper in the back of her mind, guiding her, telling her what the words meant.

"It says...'**The light has chosen the bearers.**'" Naomi paused, her heart racing. "'**The Chronicles**

of Light shall guide them through the shadows. Their path is written in faith.'"

Luke stepped back, his face paling. "That doesn't sound like a good thing."

Naomi swallowed hard, the weight of the book suddenly heavy in her hands. "I don't think we're in danger," she said, though she wasn't entirely sure. There was something powerful in this book, something that felt old and wise. It was calling to her, pulling her deeper into its mystery.

Luke ran a hand through his hair, pacing in the small space. "Naomi, this is nuts. We should put it back. We don't know what we're messing with."

But Naomi's curiosity was stronger than her fear. She knelt on the cold stone floor, placing the book on her lap. The glow flickered gently, like the steady flame of a candle, and the pages fluttered, as if inviting her to keep reading.

"There's more," she said, her voice soft. "It's like... it's telling us something."

Luke stopped pacing, his eyes darting between her and the book. "What else does it say?"

Naomi took a deep breath, her fingers trembling as she turned the page. More words began to write themselves across the parchment, glowing with the same faint light. She felt a strange connection to the book, like it was speaking to her soul, not just her mind.

"It says... **'The world's light fades, but not all is lost. The bearers must travel through time, through space, to protect the light from darkn ess.'**" Naomi paused, her heart pounding louder. **"'They are chosen to walk with the heroes of faith, to guard the light of hope.'"**

Luke stared at her, his expression unreadable. "Guard the light of hope? What does that even mean?"

Naomi's head spun with the weight of the words. Heroes of faith? Time and space? It sounded impossible, like something out of a story. But then again, here she was, holding a glowing book in a forgotten chapel in the middle of the woods. Reality was quickly starting to feel a lot more flexible.

"I think…" she started, glancing at Luke, "I think this book is asking us to do something."

Luke threw his hands up, exasperated. "Do what? Protect the light? How? We're just kids!"

Naomi opened her mouth to answer, but before she could, the ground beneath them rumbled softly, like a distant tremor. The book's light flared again, brighter this time, and the air around them thickened. Naomi felt a strange pull, like something was wrapping around her, drawing her in.

"Naomi, what's happening?" Luke's voice was edged with panic now, his eyes wide as he stumbled back.

The glow around the book intensified, and suddenly, the chapel felt smaller, the walls closing in. The light swirled around them, golden threads of energy weaving through the air, pulling at them like invisible hands.

"I don't know!" Naomi shouted, clutching the book tightly. "But I think... I think it's taking us somewhere!"

Luke's face went pale. "Taking us? Where?"

Before Naomi could respond, the world around them blurred, the stone walls of the chapel dissolving into light. The forest, the chapel, the ground beneath their feet—it all vanished in a swirl of glowing mist, and suddenly, they were weightless, spinning through a void of golden light.

Naomi gasped, her heart thundering in her chest. She could feel Luke beside her, but everything else was gone. The light was everywhere, surrounding them, filling them, and for a split second, she wondered if they had just stepped into another world.

Then, as quickly as it had begun, the swirling light stopped. The world came back into focus, but it wasn't the ruined chapel they saw.

They were standing in a city, but it was unlike any city Naomi had ever seen. The buildings were ancient, their stone walls towering above, and the streets were filled with people dressed in long robes, their faces tense with fear. Overhead, the sky was dark, and the distant sound of marching soldiers echoed through the narrow streets.

Naomi's breath caught in her throat.

"This isn't home," Luke whispered, his voice shaky. "Naomi... where are we?"

Naomi gripped the book tighter, her eyes wide as she took in the unfamiliar surroundings. She didn't know where they were. But deep down, she had a feeling the answer was written in the pages of the book.

And they were about to find out.

3

A World Unknown

THE AIR WAS THICK with tension, and Naomi could hear the faint sounds of clattering armor and hurried footsteps echoing off the stone walls of the city. It was like stepping into a living history book, except this wasn't just a story—it was real. Her heart pounded, the book still glowing faintly in her hands. She took in the narrow streets, the ancient buildings, and the sea of worried faces moving past them.

Luke stood beside her, his expression a mix of awe and fear. "Naomi, this isn't right. This... this can't be real." He looked around, his eyes darting from one strange detail to another. The robes, the soldiers, the sky darkened by smoke—none of it matched anything they knew.

Naomi didn't answer right away. She was too overwhelmed by the sheer unfamiliarity of it all. The city looked ancient, and yet it felt… alive. It was bustling with activity, but not in the joyful, vibrant way of Everbrook's busy streets. No, here, fear hung in the air like a thick fog.

"We have to figure out where we are," Naomi finally whispered, more to herself than to Luke. "And why we're here."

Luke ran a hand through his messy hair, his voice tight. "Do you think it's something to do with that book? I mean, it's the only thing that makes sense… if any of this makes sense."

Naomi looked down at the book in her hands, the glow of the ink now fading to a faint shimmer. The pages were still warm, as if the energy from before hadn't entirely left it. She had no idea what kind of power the book held, but it was clear that it had brought them here—for a reason.

As they stood there, watching people rush by, a man in a simple robe nearly collided with them. He glanced at Naomi and Luke, eyes wide with surprise and suspicion.

"You two," he hissed, grabbing Naomi's arm. "What are you doing standing here? Get inside before they find you!"

Naomi tensed, pulling her arm back. "Who? What are you talking about?"

The man's gaze flicked to the street behind them, where a group of soldiers in glinting armor marched past, their faces hard and unyielding. The man turned back to Naomi, his voice lowering to a whisper. "The Roman soldiers. You're Christians, aren't you? Don't you know what's happening?"

"Christians?" Luke's voice was a squeak, his face draining of color. "Wait—are we... are we in ancient Rome?"

Naomi's mind raced, the man's words swirling around her. Christians. Roman soldiers. It was impossible... wasn't it? But then, nothing about the last hour had been remotely possible. Her eyes fell back to the book.

Was this what it had meant?

Were they supposed to protect something here?

Before she could ask more questions, the man pushed them toward a small alleyway, his voice urgent. "You have to hide. The soldiers are searching for Christians. If they find you, they'll take you to the dungeons—or worse."

Naomi's pulse quickened as the gravity of their situation sank in. This wasn't just some adventure. They were in real danger.

Luke looked ready to bolt, his eyes wide with panic. "Naomi, we need to get out of here. Now."

But Naomi stood firm, clutching the book to her chest. There was a reason they were here. She could feel it deep inside, a stirring that wouldn't go away. "We can't leave," she said, her voice shaking but determined. "The book brought us here for a reason. We have to help."

"Help?" Luke stared at her like she'd lost her mind. "Naomi, we're just kids! What are we supposed to do, fight the Roman army?"

"No," Naomi said, glancing down at the glowing pages. "But maybe there's something else. Something we're supposed to do."

The man tugged at her arm again, his expression desperate. "Please, you don't understand. If they find you—"

"They won't," Naomi interrupted, her voice suddenly firm. "We'll hide. But first, tell us what's happening. Why are the soldiers after Christians?"

The man's face softened, and for a moment, Naomi saw something flicker in his eyes—hope. He nodded and led them deeper into the alley, where the shadows hid them from view.

"My name is Marcio," he said, his voice low. "I'm part of a small group of Christians who meet in secret. The emperor has outlawed our faith. Anyone who's caught worshipping the Lord is arrested, tortured, or worse."

Naomi's heart twisted at his words. She had learned about the persecution of early Christians in history class, but hearing it spoken by someone living through it made it real in a way she'd never imagined.

"How are you surviving?" Luke asked, his voice a little steadier now that they were out of sight.

Marcio sighed, glancing around to make sure no one else was nearby. "We have safe houses—places we can hide. But it's not enough. Every day, more of our people are taken."

Naomi's hands tightened around the book. The weight of their mission settled over her like a heavy cloak. The pages had said they were chosen to protect the light of hope, but how? What could they possibly do to help?

"We have to hide you," Marcus said again, his voice urgent. "The soldiers are ruthless."

Naomi met his eyes, her resolve hardening. "Take us to where your people are hiding. We can help."

Marcio hesitated, his brow furrowed. "Help? You're just children."

Naomi lifted the book, the faint glow catching his attention. "We're not just children. We were sent here for a reason."

For a long moment, Marcus stared at the book, his eyes wide with awe. Then, slowly, he nodded. "Follow me."

Naomi and Luke exchanged a glance. Luke's face was still pale, but he gave her a small nod. Together, they followed Marcus deeper into the maze of alleyways, the sound of soldiers' footsteps growing fainter behind them.

As they walked, Naomi's mind raced. This was real. This was happening. And somehow, they had been sent here to protect these people—people who had no one else to turn to. She didn't know how they were going to do it, but one thing was certain.

The Chronicles of Light had chosen them. And they couldn't turn back now.

4

Into the Shadows

THE WINDING ALLEYWAYS OF the ancient city seemed endless, each one darker and narrower than the last. Naomi and Luke stayed close behind Marcio, who moved swiftly, his eyes darting to every shadow as if he expected Roman soldiers to leap out at any moment. The tension was suffocating, the narrow streets closing in on them as they ventured deeper into the heart of the city.

Naomi's grip on the book tightened. Its faint glow was barely noticeable now, but she could still feel the strange energy pulsing from it, like a heartbeat. The deeper they went, the more Naomi felt a gnawing sense of responsibility settle in her chest. This wasn't just about them anymore. They were in the middle of something much bigger than she had ever imagined.

Luke, usually the voice of reason—or doubt—had been quiet for the past several minutes. Naomi glanced at him, his face set in a determined frown, eyes scanning the streets. Despite the fear she knew he felt, there was a quiet strength in him. He hadn't turned back, even though he'd had every reason to.

"We're almost there," Marcio said over his shoulder, his voice barely above a whisper. His pace quickened as they rounded a corner, and suddenly, they were standing in front of a heavy wooden door set into the stone wall of an unremarkable building.

Marcio knocked three times, his hand steady. Naomi held her breath. A tense silence hung in the air, broken only by the distant sounds of soldiers patrolling the streets. Finally, the door creaked open, revealing a woman with wide, fearful eyes. She glanced at Marcio, her gaze flickering to Naomi and Luke, and then back to Marcio.

"Who are they?" she asked, her voice laced with suspicion.

"They're here to help," Marcio said, stepping inside and motioning for Naomi and Luke to follow. "They're not like anyone we've met before."

Naomi swallowed hard as they entered the dimly lit room. The air was thick with the smell of burning oil from a few flickering lamps scattered around. Inside, huddled together in small groups, were men, women, and children, their faces drawn with fear and exhaustion. The room was no larger than a classroom back in Everbrook, but it was packed with people. Naomi's heart ached as she looked at them. These weren't just faceless characters in a history book. They were real, living people, hiding for their lives.

The door shut behind them with a heavy thud, and the woman—her face still etched with wariness—locked it with trembling hands. Marcus whispered something to her, and she nodded, casting a final, uncertain glance at Naomi and Luke before disappearing into the crowd.

Naomi turned to Marcio, her voice low. "What now?"

Marcio sighed, running a hand through his dark hair. "Now, we wait. The soldiers patrol in shifts. We can't risk moving anyone until the streets are clear."

Luke shifted uneasily beside Naomi. "How long do we have to wait?"

Marcio shrugged. "An hour, maybe more. We move when it's safe, not a moment before."

Naomi nodded, though her stomach twisted with the thought of staying in this cramped, airless room for that long. The weight of the book in her hands seemed to grow heavier with each passing moment. She knew there was more they were supposed to do—more than just hiding.

She glanced at Luke, who was fidgeting with his shirt sleeve, clearly uncomfortable in the crowded space. "We need to figure out why we're here," Naomi whispered to him. "There has to be something we're supposed to do."

Luke raised an eyebrow. "You mean other than avoid getting arrested by Roman soldiers?"

Naomi shot him a look, but before she could say anything, the book in her hands began to glow once more. She felt it before she saw it—a soft warmth spreading from the pages, just like before. She looked down in surprise as the faint light illuminated her face.

Luke noticed immediately, his eyes widening. "Naomi... your book."

The glow intensified, and Naomi felt the same pull as before, a deep sense of connection to the words forming on the page. The letters twisted and shifted, just like in the chapel, transforming from an ancient script into something she could read. Her heart raced as the words came into focus.

"The light must be protected. Find the sanctuary beneath. The bearers shall lead the way."

Naomi's breath caught in her throat as she read the words aloud, her voice trembling. The room seemed to still, the quiet murmur of voices fading as if the world around them had paused.

Luke blinked, shaking his head. "The sanctuary beneath? What does that even mean?"

Naomi bit her lip, her mind racing. "I don't know. But the book... it's telling us where to go."

Marcio stepped forward, his eyes narrowing as he stared at the glowing pages. "A sanctuary beneath?" He seemed to be thinking hard, as though trying to recall something long forgotten. Finally, his face lit up with recognition. "There's an old catacomb beneath the city. It's where we used to meet before the soldiers raided it. No one's been down there in months. It might be our only chance."

Naomi felt a surge of hope. The book hadn't led them astray yet. If it said there was a sanctuary beneath the city, then that's where they needed to go. But even as her excitement grew, doubt gnawed at the edges of her mind.

"Is it safe?" she asked, her voice quiet.

Marcio hesitated, his eyes dark with worry. "It's dangerous. The soldiers know about the catacombs, but they rarely search the lower levels. If we're careful, we can make it."

Naomi glanced at Luke, who looked like he was on the verge of protesting. She could see the worry in his eyes, the same fear that gripped her heart. But she also saw something else—trust. He trusted her. He always had, even when he didn't want to admit it.

"I think we have to go," Naomi said softly. "The book brought us here for a reason. If it says the sanctuary is beneath the city, then we need to find it."

Luke let out a long breath, running a hand through his hair. "Okay," he muttered, though his voice lacked its usual bravado. "Okay, we'll go. But if this ends with us being arrested by Roman soldiers, I'm blaming you."

Naomi couldn't help but smile, even in the middle of all the tension. "Deal."

Marcio motioned for them to follow him to the far side of the room, where a large wooden hatch lay hidden beneath a rug. He knelt down, pulling the rug aside and lifting the hatch to reveal a set of narrow stone steps descending into darkness.

"This is the way," he said, his voice low. "Once we're down there, we have to move quickly. If the soldiers find us..." His words trailed off, but Naomi didn't need him to finish. She knew the risks.

Taking a deep breath, she tightened her grip on the book and stepped toward the opening. Luke was right behind her, his footsteps hesitant but steady.

As they descended into the darkness, Naomi's mind swirled with questions. What exactly was waiting for them in the catacombs? Why had the book chosen them? And more importantly—how were they supposed to protect the light?

Whatever the answers were, she knew one thing for sure. They couldn't turn back now.

5

Into the Catacombs

The stone steps beneath Naomi's feet were cool, each one descending deeper into the earth. The narrow passage around them grew darker, the flickering light of their torches barely cutting through the suffocating blackness. Marcio led the way, his face tense as he navigated the steep and uneven terrain of the ancient catacombs beneath Rome.

Naomi's grip on the glowing book tightened with each step. It felt heavier now, as if it understood the gravity of their situation. Luke followed behind her, his footsteps hesitant, but steady, despite the palpable fear hanging in the air. The further they went, the more Naomi felt a quiet unease settling deep inside her. This was no longer just an escape—it was a journey into something ancient, something dangerous.

Marcio stopped suddenly, holding up a hand to signal them to pause. "We're close now," he whispered, his voice barely carrying over the faint sound of their breathing. "But we have to be careful. The catacombs are like a maze. It's easy to get lost."

Naomi glanced at Luke, whose face was pale in the dim light. He hadn't spoken much since they had entered the underground tunnels, and Naomi could tell that the fear was starting to get to him. It was getting to her too, but the strange energy from the book kept her moving forward. She could feel it—something was waiting for them.

The walls around them were marked with symbols—fish etched into the stone, faintly illuminated by the torchlight. Naomi's eyes lingered on one of the symbols. The ichthys, the fish symbol, a secret sign early Christians used to identify each other during times of persecution. She had learned about it in Sunday school, but seeing it here, carved into these ancient walls, felt surreal.

"These symbols..." Luke whispered, his voice shaky, "they're everywhere."

Naomi nodded, her eyes tracing the ancient carvings. "It's a sign for Christians," she said quietly, her fingers brushing against one of the etched fish. "It means they've been here, hiding, worshipping in secret."

Marcio glanced over his shoulder, his face solemn. "This is where we used to meet, before the soldiers began raiding the catacombs. These symbols were our guide to safety."

They continued down the winding tunnels, the air growing colder and thicker with the scent of earth and stone. Every now and then, Naomi would catch sight of more symbols carved into the walls—crosses, the letters XP for Christ, and small, hastily scratched drawings that seemed to tell stories of faith and hope. The deeper they went, the more Naomi's heart ached for the people who had once gathered here, risking everything to worship in secret.

Marcio led them to a larger chamber, its high, vaulted ceiling giving the impression of a hidden sanctuary. The flicker of their torches revealed rows of stone benches, and in the center of the room stood a small altar, covered with dust but still intact. Naomi could almost imagine the faint echoes of whispered prayers and hymns filling the air, the quiet courage of those who gathered here in defiance of the Roman Empire.

"This is where they met," Marcio said, his voice soft and reverent. "My family... all of us. We would come here to pray, to find peace."

Naomi's heart squeezed in her chest. The reality of their situation was sinking in deeper now. These were real people—families just like hers, only separated by centuries. And yet, their faith had been the same.

Luke stepped closer to the altar, his eyes wide as he scanned the room. "It's hard to believe people risked their lives to come here," he murmured, his voice thick with emotion. "For their faith."

"They did," Marcio replied quietly. "And many still do."

Naomi ran her fingers over the surface of the book, feeling the warmth pulse through it again. She couldn't help but wonder—why had the book brought them here? What were they supposed to do in this ancient place, where fear and faith collided in the shadows of history?

As if in response to her unspoken question, the book began to glow once more. Naomi's breath hitched, and she opened it carefully, the pages flick-ering with light as new words formed before her eyes.

"The light must not fade. Protect the flame of faith. You are the bearers of the light, chosen to shield it from the darkness."

Naomi's pulse quickened as she read the words aloud, her voice trembling. She didn't understand what the book was telling her—how could they, two kids from Everbrook, be responsible for protecting something so ancient and sacred?

Luke stepped closer, his gaze fixed on the glowing pages. "What does it mean?" he asked, his voice low. "How are we supposed to protect anything? We don't even know what we're doing here."

Naomi swallowed hard, her eyes locked on the book. "I don't know," she admitted. "But I think we're supposed to do something here—something important."

Marcio, who had been listening intently, stepped forward. His face was pale but determined. "If the book says you're here to protect the light, then there must be a reason. This sanctuary... it was once a refuge, but now it's a symbol. A symbol of our faith, of the hope we still carry, even in the face of fear."

Naomi's heart ached at his words. She could feel the weight of responsibility settling over her like a heavy cloak. They were here for a reason. They couldn't leave without doing what they had been sent to do.

Before she could respond, the sound of distant footsteps echoed through the tunnels. Naomi's breath caught in her throat. Roman soldiers—they were getting closer.

"They've found us," Marcio whispered, his face tense. "We have to hide."

Panic surged in Naomi's chest, but she forced herself to stay calm. "Where can we go?"

Marcio motioned to a small passage hidden be-hind the altar. "There's a lower level of the cata-combs—deeper, harder to navigate. They won't find us there."

Naomi nodded, grabbing Luke's arm and pulling him toward the hidden passage. Her heart was pounding in her ears as they slipped through the narrow opening, the sounds of the soldiers' foot-steps growing louder.

As they descended deeper into the catacombs, the light from their torches barely illuminated the way. The air grew colder, and the tunnels more cramped, but they kept moving. Naomi could feel the book pulsing in her hands, its glow dimming as they pressed on.

Finally, they reached a small alcove, barely large enough for the three of them to hide. Marcio crouched down beside them, his breathing shallow as he listened for any sign of the soldiers.

Naomi's mind raced, her pulse thudding in her throat. The book had brought them here for a reason, but what were they supposed to do now? How could they protect the light, when it felt like they were the ones in need of protection?

In the silence, she closed her eyes and whispered a prayer. "Help us Lord. Show us the way."

A soft warmth spread through her, and when she opened her eyes, the book in her hands glowed faintly once more. The words on the page shifted, new instructions forming in the light.

"The sanctuary must be kept hidden. The way forward is not through battle, but through faith. Trust the light. It will guide you."

Naomi's breath caught in her throat. Trust the light. It was the only way.

She turned to Marcio and Luke, her voice steady despite the fear gnawing at her. "We have to trust the light. The book... it's telling us what to do."

Luke frowned, his brow furrowed. "But what does that mean? How are we supposed to trust it?"

"I don't know," Naomi admitted. "But I think it means we're not supposed to fight. We're supposed to protect the sanctuary by keeping it hidden—by trusting that the light will guide us."

Marcio nodded slowly, his face pale but resolute. "Then we will trust."

The footsteps of the soldiers drew nearer, but Naomi's heart remained steady. The light would guide them—she knew it now, with a certainty she couldn't explain. They were the bearers of the light, and somehow, they would find a way to protect it.

Together, they waited in the silence of the cata-combs, trusting in the light to lead them through the darkness. Suddenly a young boy, no older than twelve, darted around the corner, his chest rising and falling quickly, his face pale with fear. He wore a simple tunic, and his sandals slapped against the stone floor as he ran.

The boy's eyes widened when he saw them. For a brief moment, Naomi wondered if he would run away, but then his gaze landed on the book in her hands, and something flickered across his face—recognition, hope.

"Come with me!" the boy whispered urgently, his eyes darting to the tunnel behind him. "Quickly, before they find us!"

Naomi hesitated for only a second before nodding. She glanced at Luke, whose expression was a mix of confusion and fear, and motioned for him and

Marcio to follow. Together, they ran after the boy, deeper into the twisting catacombs.

They followed him through a labyrinth of tunnels, barely catching their breath. Finally, the boy stopped in front of a small alcove carved into the stone. Naomi noticed other figures huddled there—a man and a woman, both dressed in worn clothing, their faces tense with worry. The man, his brow furrowed, held a small child close to his chest.

The boy stepped forward, his voice trembling. "This is my family. We have been here since the last raid, hiding from the soldiers."

Naomi's breath caught in her throat as she looked at the boy's family. She could see the exhaustion in their eyes, the fear etched into their faces. She had read about the persecution of Christians in ancient Rome, how they were hunted for their faith and forced to hide in these catacombs. But seeing it—feeling it—was entirely different.

"My name is Marcus," the boy continued, his eyes now fixed on Naomi and Luke. "We've been hiding here for months, but the soldiers are going to start looking here again soon. I don't know how much longer we can stay."

Naomi's heart ached as she looked at Marcus and his family. They were just trying to survive, holding on to their faith even in the face of death. How could anyone stay strong in the midst of such fear? Her own faith, something that had always been so sure, suddenly felt fragile.

Luke, who had been silent, stepped forward. "Why are they after you?"

Marcio stepped forward and exchanged a glance with Marcus's father before answering. "Because we follow Christ. In Rome, the emperor is worshipped as a god, and anyone who refuses is seen as a traitor. Christians are... enemies of the state."

Naomi felt a chill run down her spine. The gravity of the situation sank in—these people were risking their lives, their children's lives, for their faith. She thought of her own family, her father preaching freely in their church back home. How easy her faith had been compared to this.

Suddenly, a sharp clatter echoed down the tunnel, followed by muffled voices. Naomi's heart leapt into her throat.

"The soldiers," Marcus whispered, his face pale. "They're coming."

6

The Escape

THE STONE WALLS OF the catacombs pressed in on them as they hurried through the narrow passageways, the faint flicker of their torches barely cutting through the oppressive darkness. Naomi's breath came in shallow bursts, her heart pounding as she struggled to keep up with Marcus. Behind her, Luke, Marcus's family, and Marcio followed closely, their footsteps quickened by the fear of the approaching Roman soldiers.

Naomi clutched the glowing book tightly to her chest, its soft warmth the only comfort in the cold, damp tunnel. Every step seemed to echo with urgency as they fled deeper into the ancient underground maze, the sound of Roman soldiers' foot-steps growing louder in the distance.

Marcus glanced back at them, his face tense. "We're close now," he whispered. "There's a passage up ahead that leads to the lower levels. If we can reach it, we might be safe—for now."

Naomi nodded, though a knot of anxiety twisted in her stomach. She could feel the weight of the responsibility pressing down on her—this wasn't just an escape. The book had brought them here for a reason, and they hadn't yet discovered what that reason was. Somehow, they were supposed to protect the light, to help these people, but how?

Luke, sensing her tension, leaned in. "Naomi, what are we supposed to do? We can't outrun them forever."

She met his eyes, her mind racing. "I don't know," she admitted, her voice barely above a whisper.

"But the book—it brought us here for a reason. We just have to trust that it'll show us the way."

Luke frowned, clearly not satisfied with that answer, but before he could say anything, Marcus stopped suddenly in front of a small opening barely visible against the stone wall.

"Through here," Marcus whispered, motioning for them to enter. "It's tight, but it leads to a hidden chamber. They won't find us there."

Naomi swallowed hard as she squeezed through the narrow gap, her heart pounding in her chest. Luke followed close behind, his breath coming in quick, nervous bursts. Marcus's family, including his mother, father, and younger sister, moved silently as well. Marcio stayed near the back, his face set in a determined frown as he scanned the dark tunnels for any sign of pursuit. As they crawled deeper into the crevice, the tunnel grew colder, the air thick with the scent of earth and stone. The darkness pressed in on them from all sides, and for a moment, Naomi's fear threatened to overwhelm her.

But then, the book in her hands pulsed softly, its glow cutting through the blackness. The warmth from its pages calmed her racing thoughts, reminding her that they weren't alone. They had been chosen for this—for a reason.

Once inside the hidden chamber, everyone crouched down, holding their breath. The glow of the book was the only source of light as Marcus pressed his ear to the stone wall, listening for the soldiers. The distant clang of armor echoed faintly through the tunnels, growing louder with each passing moment.

"They're close," Marcus whispered, his face pale. "If they find us..."

"They won't," Naomi said, her voice more certain than she felt. She clutched the book tightly, hoping it would provide them with the answers they so desperately needed.

Luke shot her a worried glance. "What are we supposed to do? We're not warriors. We can't fight them."

Naomi stared at the glowing book in her hands, its light flickering softly in the dim chamber. The words that had appeared earlier swirled in her mind: The light must not fade. Protect the flame of faith.

"I don't think we're supposed to fight," Naomi said quietly. "The book said something about protecting the flame of faith. I think we're supposed to hide it, to keep it safe."

"But how?" Marcus's father, his face etched with worry, asked. "How do we protect something like that when we're the ones being hunted?"

Before Naomi could answer, the sound of approaching footsteps grew louder, reverberating through the stone walls. The soldiers were near.

"Trust the light," Naomi murmured, almost to herself. The words had come from the book before, and though she didn't fully understand their meaning, she felt the truth in them. They weren't supposed to fight. They were supposed to protect.

As if responding to her thoughts, the book began to glow brighter, its warmth spreading through her hands. Naomi's breath hitched, and she opened it carefully, the pages flickering with light as new words formed before her eyes.

The sanctuary must remain hidden. The way forward is through faith, not battle. Trust in the light. It will guide you.

Naomi read the words aloud, her voice trembling. Luke, Marcus, Marcio, and the others listened intently, their expressions a mix of awe and confusion.

"What does it mean?" Luke asked, his brow furrowed. "How do we trust the light?"

Before Naomi could respond, the glow from the book grew even brighter, illuminating the entire chamber with a soft, golden light. The air around them seemed to hum with energy, and Naomi could feel the pulse of the book growing stronger in her hands.

Marcus stared at the light, his face pale with awe. "This is a sign," he whispered, his voice trembling. "The light...it's protecting us."

Naomi nodded, her heart racing. "We have to trust it," she said softly. "We can't fight the soldiers. But the light—it will guide us to safety."

Marcus's father, his face pale but resolute, nodded in agreement. "Then we trust the light."

The group huddled together in the small chamber, the glow from the book casting long shadows on the walls. The sound of the soldiers grew louder, their footsteps echoing through the tunnels, but the light around them remained steady. It was as if the soldiers' presence couldn't penetrate the sanctuary the book had created.

Minutes passed, though it felt like hours. The soldiers' footsteps drew closer, then slowly faded as they moved deeper into the catacombs, unaware of the small, hidden chamber just out of sight.

When the last echoes of armor finally disappeared, Marcus let out a shaky breath. "They're gone," he whispered, his voice thick with relief.

Naomi closed the book, the glow dimming as the immediate danger passed. Her heart pounded in her chest, but the sense of peace that had settled over them remained. They had trusted the light, and it had protected them.

"We did it," Luke whispered, his eyes wide with disbelief. "We actually survived."

Marcus's mother, tears in her eyes, nodded in agreement. "The Lord has delivered us," she said softly, her voice filled with gratitude.

Naomi nodded, though her thoughts were already racing ahead. The danger had passed, but their mission wasn't over. The book had brought them here for a reason—to protect something far greater than themselves.

Suddenly, the glow from the book flared to life once more, brighter than ever before. Naomi's breath caught in her throat as she felt the familiar tugging sensation in her chest—the same feeling she had when they had first been transported to Rome.

"No..." she whispered, glancing at Luke, Marcus, and the others. "Not yet. We haven't—"

But it was too late. The light from the book engulfed them all, swirling around them in a whirlwind of gold and white. The ground beneath them disappeared, and the room—the catacombs, Marcus, his family, Marcio, the sanctuary—faded away into a blur of light and sound.

They were being transported again.

The familiar spinning sensation returned, the world twisting and dissolving into a cascade of colors and light. Naomi clutched the book tightly, her mind racing as the reality of their situation settled over her. They had done something important here—helped keep the faith alive in this ancient, dangerous place. But whatever they were meant to do, it wasn't over.

As the world around them spun, she glanced at Luke. His eyes were wide, but there was a determination in them now that hadn't been there before—a shared understanding between them all. Whatever came next, they would face it together.

The swirling light slowly faded, and Naomi felt solid ground beneath her feet once more. The world came back into focus—new surroundings, unfamiliar yet waiting to be explored. The hum of the book settled, and the glow dimmed, leaving only the quiet anticipation of what lay ahead.

Their journey wasn't over.

7

A Warriors Doubt

The ground beneath Naomi's feet felt solid again as the whirlwind of light finally faded. She blinked, her vision slowly adjusting to their new surroundings. The air was cool, heavy with the scent of damp earth, smoke, and something that felt distinctly old, as if history itself clung to the wind. Trees stretched high above them, their dense foliage forming a canopy that blocked most of the sunlight, casting everything in a shadowy green hue.

Naomi steadied herself, gripping the book tightly as its glow dimmed. She glanced around, taking in the unfamiliar landscape. They stood in the midst of a thick forest, and in the distance, the faint outline of a village could be seen nestled against rolling hills. The architecture was unmistakably medieval—simple wooden houses with thatched roofs, and far beyond the village, perched on a hill, a grand stone fortress loomed.

Luke staggered beside her, still recovering from the transport. "Are we... in France?" he asked, his voice laced with confusion as he surveyed the surroundings.

Naomi nodded, though her heart pounded in her chest. "I think so. But not just any part of France... I think we've gone back to medieval times."

The realization hit hard. Naomi had always loved history, but being thrust into it was an entirely different experience. The faint clang of metal and the distant murmur of voices carried through the trees, and the tension in the air felt almost tangible, like something monumental was about to happen.

Before Naomi could voice her thoughts, the sound of hoofbeats broke through the forest, growing louder with every passing second. Naomi and Luke turned toward the noise just as a figure on horseback emerged from the trees. A girl, no older than sixteen, her face sharp with focus and determination, rode toward them. She was dressed in a suit of armor, though it looked oversized, as if it had been hastily fitted. In her hand, she carried a banner—a white flag adorned with a golden cross and sword, fluttering in the wind.

Naomi's heart stopped. She knew who this was, even before the girl spoke.

"It's her," Naomi whispered, her voice filled with awe. "Joan of Arc."

Luke's eyes widened in disbelief. "You mean the Joan of Arc? The one who led armies and fought for France?"

Naomi nodded, too stunned to speak further. The figure before them was both legendary and real, her face familiar from countless books and stories, yet now filled with the kind of emotion that no history book could capture. Joan's features were a mix of strength and vulnerability, her youthful face lined with the weight of responsibility far beyond her years.

Joan slowed her horse to a stop a few feet away, her sharp eyes sweeping over them. For a moment, her expression softened, curiosity flickering across her face as she studied Naomi and Luke, their modern clothes standing out against the backdrop of her world.

"Who are you?" Joan demanded, her voice firm yet carrying a trace of uncertainty. Her hand rested lightly on the hilt of her sword. "What are you doing here?"

Naomi's throat tightened. She wasn't sure how to explain—how could she tell Joan that they had been transported through time to help her, that they had been sent on a mission to protect the light of faith? Her mind raced for the right words.

"We're not from here," Naomi said carefully, her voice steady but cautious. "But we were sent to help you."

Joan's gaze sharpened, her eyes narrowing with suspicion. She sat tall in her saddle, her posture radiating authority despite the doubt that flickered in her eyes. "Sent by whom?" she asked, her tone edged with skepticism.

Naomi glanced at Luke, who gave her an encouraging nod. She took a deep breath, feeling the weight of the book in her hands. "By God," Naomi said softly, meeting Joan's intense gaze. "We were sent to help you, just like you were sent to help France."

Joan's brow furrowed, and for a moment, Naomi thought she might reject their story outright. But instead, Joan's grip on her sword tightened, and her gaze flickered with something Naomi hadn't expected—uncertainty. Joan's legendary bravery had been immortalized in history books, but standing before them now, she looked like a girl burdened by doubt.

"If you were sent by God," Joan said, her voice quieter now, "then tell me why I can no longer hear Him. Why has His voice left me?"

Naomi's heart ached at the raw vulnerability in Joan's words. This was why they had been brought here—not to witness Joan's triumphs, but to help her through her struggle. The girl who had claimed to hear divine voices, the fearless leader of armies, was now questioning her faith.

"You're doubting," Naomi said softly, stepping forward, careful not to startle Joan or her horse.

Joan's jaw tightened, her eyes flashing with something close to anger. "How can I not doubt? God chose me—me, a simple girl from a village, to lead France. He gave me visions, and I followed them. But now..." Her voice faltered, and she looked away, her shoulders tense. "Now, His voice is silent. I wonder if I've failed Him, if I am not worthy of this mission after all."

Naomi felt a deep sense of empathy for Joan. She had read about Joan's unwavering faith, how she had believed with every fiber of her being that she was chosen by God to save France. But now, standing before them, Joan was just a young girl, burdened with the impossible task of saving a country, her belief shaken by the weight of responsibility.

"You haven't failed," Naomi said gently. "Everyone has moments of doubt, even when they know they're on the right path. It doesn't mean you're not worthy."

Joan looked back at her, her eyes searching Naomi's face as if trying to understand how someone who seemed so ordinary could know anything about what she was going through. "How can I be sure?" Joan asked, her voice quiet and uncertain. "How can I know that I am still following God's will when I can no longer hear His voice?"

Naomi swallowed hard, the gravity of Joan's question sinking in. She didn't have all the answers, but she felt a strange sense of clarity. The book in her hands pulsed softly, its warmth spreading through her fingers as if urging her to speak.

"Sometimes," Naomi began, choosing her words carefully, "faith isn't about hearing God's voice clearly. It's about trusting that He's still with you, even in the silence. You were chosen for this mission, Joan. That hasn't changed just because it's hard now. God hasn't left you. You just have to trust that He's guiding you, even when you can't hear Him."

Joan's eyes softened, her fierce exterior cracking just slightly. For a moment, the girl who had led armies, who had faced overwhelming odds, looked like a frightened child seeking reassurance.

"How do you know?" Joan asked, her voice barely above a whisper.

Naomi hesitated. How could she explain that her own journey, though not as monumental as Joan's, had been filled with doubt too? She had faced moments where she wondered if she was strong enough to follow God's will, moments where she felt lost and uncertain. But those moments hadn't made her faith weaker—they had made it stronger.

"I know because I've felt it too," Naomi said quietly. "Doubt doesn't mean your faith is gone. It just means you're human. But the fact that you're still here, still fighting—that means your faith is stronger than you think."

Joan's gaze held hers for a long moment, and then, slowly, Joan nodded. The tension in her shoulders seemed to ease, and her grip on her sword relaxed.

"I have doubted," Joan admitted, her voice softening. "But you're right. I cannot let that doubt stop me from fulfilling the mission God gave me. I will trust that He is still with me, even in the silence."

Luke, who had been watching the exchange in silence, stepped forward. "You've already done so much, Joan. You believed when no one else did. That's why people follow you. You have to keep believing."

Joan looked at him, a small smile tugging at the corners of her lips. "Perhaps I have forgotten that belief is what brought me this far. Thank you," she said, her voice filled with renewed determination.

"I must return to my men. There is a battle ahead, and I cannot waver."

Naomi nodded, her heart swelling with admiration for Joan. This girl, who had faced unimaginable challenges and carried the weight of a nation on her shoulders, was choosing to trust her faith even when it seemed most difficult.

As Joan mounted her horse, her banner fluttering in the wind once more, she looked down at Naomi and Luke. "You may not be from here, but you have reminded me of something I had nearly forgotten. God is with me, even when I do not hear His voice. I will trust in that."

Naomi smiled, relief washing over her. They had helped Joan, but more than that, they had witnessed her strength firsthand. Joan's bravery was more than just leading armies—it was about having the courage to trust in her calling, even when the path seemed uncertain.

As Joan rode off into the distance, heading back toward the fortress and the battle that awaited her, Naomi felt a deep sense of awe. Joan had found her strength again, but Naomi couldn't shake the feeling that the lesson wasn't just for Joan—it was for her too.

Joan's courage inspired her, but it also made her question her own strength. As Joan's figure disappeared into the horizon, a wave of silence fell over the forest. The tension in the air, once thick with Joan's uncertainty, lifted, leaving Naomi standing there with the weight of her own questions. Joan had found her courage again, but Naomi couldn't ignore the lingering doubt within herself.

Luke, standing beside her, let out a long breath. "That was... intense. She's like a living legend, and she's not even sure if she can keep going."

Naomi nodded, staring at the spot where Joan had vanished. "Even heroes have doubts, I guess."

"But she's strong," Luke said, his voice thoughtful. "Stronger than I ever imagined. She's going into a battle, not knowing if she'll live or die, and she's still trusting that it's all part of some bigger plan."

Naomi shifted uneasily, feeling the familiar weight of uncertainty creep into her mind. Joan had been chosen by God to lead, but she still struggled to hear His voice. Naomi couldn't help but wonder—would she be able to do the same? Would she be brave enough to follow God's will, even if it meant walking into danger?

Luke turned toward her, his expression serious. "Naomi, you really helped her back there. You gave her hope. You told her to trust God even when things seemed impossible. But do you believe that for yourself?"

Naomi blinked, surprised by Luke's question. She had spoken from her heart when she told Joan to trust, even in the silence. But now, with the dust settling from their encounter, Naomi felt her own doubts bubbling to the surface. Could she be strong like Joan? Could she trust in God's plan, even when the path was unclear?

"I don't know," Naomi admitted, her voice barely above a whisper. "It's easy to say those things when you're helping someone else, but when it's your own life..." She trailed off, unsure of how to put her fears into words.

Luke stepped closer, his brow furrowed. "You've always been the one with faith, Naomi. You always seem so sure about God's plan. But what if..." He hesitated, his voice softening. "What if the path is dangerous? What if trusting God means risking everything? Would you still do it?"

Naomi looked down at the book in her hands, the soft glow from its pages now faded. The responsibility of being the bearer of this mysterious light felt heavier than ever. Joan had struggled with doubt, and Naomi had helped her find the strength to carry on. But Naomi hadn't expected to feel the same fear and uncertainty gnawing at her.

"I don't know," Naomi said again, her voice trembling. "I want to believe that I'd be strong enough. But if I were in Joan's place—leading armies, risking my life—what if I'm not brave enough? What if I fail?"

Luke was quiet for a moment, his gaze thoughtful. "You wouldn't fail. You always say that faith isn't about having all the answers. Maybe it's the same with courage. Maybe being brave isn't about never feeling afraid—it's about pushing through the fear anyway."

Naomi looked up at Luke, his words sinking in. He had been skeptical of faith from the start, always questioning, always doubting. But now, standing in this strange place, Luke seemed to understand something that Naomi hadn't fully grasped.

"You're right," Naomi said softly. "Maybe being brave isn't about not being afraid. Maybe it's about trusting that God will be with you, even when the path is scary."

Luke smiled slightly, the usual sarcasm absent from his voice. "Sounds like you've got it figured out."

Naomi returned the smile, though the knot of fear in her chest hadn't entirely loosened. She had seen Joan's bravery, and it had inspired her. But she also knew that walking in faith meant walking into the unknown, where the future was uncertain, and the stakes were high.

8

TRIALS OF FAITH

THE SUN DIPPED LOW on the horizon, casting a golden hue across the medieval landscape, painting the rolling hills and dense forest in shades of amber and crimson. The wind stirred, carrying the scent of wood smoke and damp earth as Naomi and Luke made their way along a narrow path, winding through the trees. The sense of something larger than themselves—something ancient and powerful—hung in the air, pressing down on them as they walked.

Naomi couldn't shake the image of Joan riding off into the distance, her banner waving defiantly in the wind. The young girl had found her courage again, rekindling her faith in a way that seemed almost supernatural. But Naomi was left grappling with her own questions—her own fears.

"Do you think she'll win?" Luke asked, breaking the silence. He walked a little behind Naomi, his eyes trained on the distant horizon, where the towering fortress still stood, barely visible in the fading light.

Naomi hesitated, turning the question over in her mind. She had studied Joan of Arc in school, knew the history of how Joan had led the French to victory in key battles during the Hundred Years' War. But she also knew that Joan's life ended in tragedy—captured by her enemies, put on trial for heresy, and burned at the stake. The weight of knowing Joan's fate gnawed at Naomi, but she wasn't sure how to answer Luke's question.

"I don't know," Naomi finally said, her voice soft. "She'll win some battles, but..." She trailed off, unsure if she should share the darker part of Joan's story. "Her story doesn't end the way we'd want it to."

Luke frowned, his face thoughtful as he processed Naomi's words. "But she still went back. She still chose to fight, even though she had doubts. She knew the risks."

"That's what makes her so brave," Naomi said, feeling a tightness in her chest. "She trusted God's plan, even when it didn't make sense. Even when she knew it could end badly for her."

Luke was quiet for a moment, his steps slowing. "I don't get it. How could anyone just...accept that? Knowing it might not end well for them? How could Joan just ride into battle, knowing what might happen?"

Naomi stopped walking and turned to face him, her brow furrowed as she searched for the right words. "Joan believed that what she was doing was bigger than herself. She knew that God had called her to lead France, to inspire her people, even if it meant sacrificing her life."

Luke stared at her, his face a mix of frustration and confusion. "But why would God ask that of her? I mean, why would He want her to do something so dangerous, knowing she might die?"

Naomi didn't have a perfect answer. She had asked herself the same question many times. But after their encounter with Joan, after witnessing her struggle with doubt and her ultimate decision to trust in her calling, Naomi realized something.

"Maybe it's not about whether God wants someone to be in danger," Naomi said slowly, her voice thoughtful. "Maybe it's about what that person is willing to do because they believe in something bigger. Joan wasn't just fighting for herself—she was fighting for her country, for her faith. She believed that her life had a purpose, even if it was danger-ous."

Luke shook his head, looking down at the ground. "I don't know if I could do that. How could anyone?"

Naomi stepped closer to him, her voice gentle. "I think it's about trust. Trusting that even when things seem impossible, God is still with you. That He has a plan, even if it's hard to understand."

Luke glanced up at her, his expression uncertain. "Do you really believe that?"

Naomi hesitated. She wanted to say yes, that she fully trusted God's plan no matter what. But the truth was, after seeing Joan's bravery, Naomi was more aware of her own fears than ever before. Joan had faced her doubts and chosen to trust, but could Naomi do the same? Could she walk a path filled with uncertainty and danger, knowing that the outcome might not be what she hoped for?

"I want to believe it," Naomi admitted, her voice soft. "But it's hard. It's scary to think about what might happen if you follow God's plan and things go wrong."

Luke nodded slowly, his gaze drifting to the horizon once more. "Yeah, it is."

They stood in silence for a while, the wind rustling the leaves overhead as the sky darkened, stars beginning to peek through the fading light. The world around them seemed to hold its breath, as if waiting for something to break the stillness.

After a few minutes, Luke spoke again, his voice quieter this time. "Do you think Joan was afraid when she went into battle? Like, even with all that faith, do you think she still felt scared?"

Naomi looked at him, her heart aching with the weight of the question. She had seen the fear in Joan's eyes, the doubt that had gripped her before Naomi and Luke helped her find her courage again.

Joan had been afraid, just like anyone would be. But she had chosen to move forward anyway.

"Yeah," Naomi said softly. "I think she was scared. But I also think that's what made her brave. She didn't let the fear stop her."

Luke nodded, a small frown tugging at the corners of his mouth. "I've never thought about faith like that. I always thought it was about being sure of everything, about not having any doubts. But maybe...maybe it's more about trusting even when you're scared."

Naomi smiled slightly, touched by Luke's words. For someone who had always been so skeptical of faith, he was beginning to understand it in a new way. She could see the change in him—his doubts were still there, but something deeper was starting to take root.

"You're right," Naomi said. "Faith isn't about having all the answers. It's about trusting even when you don't. Joan showed us that."

Luke let out a deep breath, the tension in his shoulders easing a little. "I guess we're all just trying to figure it out."

Naomi nodded, feeling the same uncertainty in her own heart. Joan's story had inspired her, but it had also reminded her that following God's will wasn't easy. It required trust, courage, and the willingness to step into the unknown, even when the outcome was uncertain.

As they continued walking, the path ahead seemed darker, more foreboding. The soft glow of the book in Naomi's hands pulsed faintly, lighting their way.

The air was cooler now, the wind picking up as night fully descended.

Suddenly, the book's faint glow began to brighten, the warmth from its pages spreading through Naomi's hands. She stopped in her tracks, and Luke turned to her, concern in his eyes.

"What's happening?" he asked.

Naomi's breath caught as the familiar energy pulsed from the book. The words on the page shifted, rearranging themselves into something new. She could feel it—the book was trying to guide them again.

"The book," Naomi whispered, her voice trembling with anticipation. "It's telling us something."

Luke stepped closer, his eyes fixed on the glowing pages. "What does it say?"

Naomi stared at the newly formed words, her heart pounding in her chest. The message was simple, yet profound:

"The light will guide you through the darkness, but you must have the courage to follow it."

Naomi's pulse quickened as she read the words aloud, her voice steady despite the fear gnawing at her insides. The message was clear—they were about to face something more, something that would test their faith even further.

Luke swallowed hard, his gaze flicking between Naomi and the glowing book. "Do you think it means what I think it means?"

Naomi nodded, her heart pounding. "It's telling us to keep moving, even though we don't know what's ahead."

Luke was quiet for a moment, processing the weight of the message. He looked up at the dark forest that lay before them, the wind howling through the trees like a warning. "Do you think we're ready?"

Naomi took a deep breath, the warmth of the book still pulsing in her hands. She didn't know if she was ready—if either of them were. But Joan had found her courage in the face of uncertainty, and Naomi knew that she had to do the same.

"I don't know," Naomi admitted. "But we have to trust the light. It's gotten us this far, hasn't it?"

Luke nodded slowly, a small smile tugging at his lips. "Yeah, it has."

Together, they continued down the path, the soft glow of the book lighting their way. The wind howled, and the darkness pressed in around them, but Naomi felt a quiet strength growing inside her. She didn't have all the answers, and the fear still lingered, but she knew one thing for certain:

They would follow the light—no matter where it led.

9

A New Light

THE NIGHT SKY HAD turned dark, with only a few stars peeking through the thick clouds overhead. The wind had grown stronger, pushing the scent of rain and earth through the forest as Naomi and Luke continued walking. The soft glow of the book had dimmed, leaving them in the fading twilight, the only sound the rustling of leaves underfoot and the distant call of the wind.

Luke had been quiet for most of the journey, his mind swirling with thoughts. Seeing Joan of Arc—seeing her courage, her doubt, and her ultimate faith—had stirred something inside him. He hadn't expected it, but watching her ride into battle despite her fear had made him question everything he thought he knew about faith, about strength, and about himself.

He glanced at Naomi, who walked a few steps ahead, her eyes focused on the path. She had always been the one with unwavering faith, the one who believed without hesitation. But now, after everything they had witnessed, Luke could see the uncertainty in her eyes. It was the same uncertainty he felt.

"Naomi," he said softly, breaking the silence. "Do you ever think that... maybe we're in over our heads?"

Naomi slowed her pace, turning to look at him. There was a flicker of doubt in her eyes, but she gave him a small, reassuring smile. "Yeah, sometimes. But I think that's part of the journey—feeling like we don't have all the answers and still choosing to trust anyway."

Luke nodded, but the weight of her words settled heavily on his heart. Trust. He had always struggled with that. How could he trust in something he couldn't see, couldn't fully understand? Joan had trusted, even when God's voice seemed distant. She had chosen to believe in something bigger than herself, even though the outcome was uncertain.

Could he do the same?

They walked in silence for a while longer, the tension between them almost palpable. The book in Naomi's hands seemed quieter now, its usual hum of energy barely noticeable. Luke couldn't help but feel that something had shifted since their encounter with Joan. It was as if the book was waiting—waiting for something new, something different.

Suddenly, Naomi stopped walking, her brow furrowing as she stared down at the book. "It's not glowing anymore," she whispered, her voice tinged with worry. "What if... what if it's done with us? What if our mission is over?"

Luke frowned, stepping closer to her. "But we haven't figured out what we're really supposed to do yet. There has to be more."

Naomi shook her head, her uncertainty growing. "I don't know. The book always lights up when it's leading us somewhere, but now... nothing."

Luke reached out, his hand brushing against the cover of the book. As soon as his fingers made contact, a jolt of warmth shot up his arm, and the soft glow returned to the pages, faint at first, but growing stronger with each passing second. Naomi's eyes widened in surprise, and Luke's heart skipped a beat.

"It's you," Naomi whispered, stepping back slightly. "The book... it's responding to you."

Luke looked down at the glowing book in his hands, his mind racing. He had never felt this connection to the book before—had never even believed it held any real power. But now, as he held it, the warmth and energy pulsing through it felt real, alive.

"Try opening it," Naomi urged, her voice filled with a mixture of curiosity and awe.

Luke hesitated for a moment, then slowly opened the book. The pages shimmered, the strange symbols that had always baffled him shifting and re-arranging themselves into words—words he could read.

His breath caught in his throat as the message on the page became clear.

"The time has come for a new bearer. The light seeks those who doubt, those who fear, and those who are called to believe. Step forward in faith, and the path will be revealed."

Luke's hands trembled as he read the words aloud. His heart pounded in his chest, the weight of what he had just read settling over him like a heavy blanket.

Naomi stared at him, her eyes wide with amazement. "Luke... you can read it. You've been chosen."

Luke shook his head, backing away slightly. "No. No, this doesn't make sense. I'm not... I'm not like you, Naomi. I don't have that kind of faith."

"But maybe that's why the book is choosing you," Naomi said softly. "You've always questioned, always doubted. Maybe that's what makes you the one who needs to carry the light now."

Luke swallowed hard, the reality of the situation pressing down on him. He had never considered himself worthy of something like this—never believed that he could be the one to carry something so important. But the book had chosen him, and now there was no turning back.

As he stared down at the glowing pages, the world around them began to shift. The ground trembled beneath their feet, and a familiar light enveloped them, swirling around in golden strands, pulling them into its embrace. The sensation of weightlessness returned, and Luke's heart raced as the world blurred and twisted around them.

"We're being transported again," Naomi whispered, her voice tight with anticipation.

Luke clutched the book tightly, his mind spinning as the light around them grew brighter, pulling them further and further from the dark forest. He could feel the power of the book coursing through him, guiding them to wherever they were meant to go next.

And then, just as quickly as it had begun, the light faded, and they found themselves standing in a new place.

The air was cool and crisp, the faint smell of smoke and metal lingering in the air. Luke blinked, trying to clear the disorientation from his mind as he took in their surroundings. They were standing in a small village, its narrow streets lined with wooden houses. In the distance, the towering silhouette of a castle loomed against the sky, its stone walls dark and imposing.

Naomi stepped forward, her eyes scanning the village with a mixture of curiosity and awe. "Where are we now?"

Luke didn't answer right away. His mind was still racing from what had just happened, from the realization that the book had chosen him, that he was now the one who had to carry this burden of light and faith.

"I don't know," he finally said, his voice quieter than he had intended. "But I guess we're about to find out."

As they stood there, trying to make sense of their new surroundings, Luke felt the book pulse in his hands once more. The glow was faint now, but the warmth was still there, a reminder that their journey was far from over.

Naomi turned to him, her expression filled with quiet strength. "You're not alone in this, Luke. We're in this together."

Luke nodded, though the weight of the book in his hands still felt overwhelming. He had always questioned faith, always doubted whether there was something greater guiding them. But now, as he held the book that had chosen him, he realized that maybe, just maybe, he was ready to believe.

The path ahead was still uncertain, and the fear still lingered. But for the first time, Luke felt a spark of hope, a glimmer of something deeper within him.

Joan's bravery had inspired him, and now it was his turn to step forward in faith.

The light would guide him—and he would follow it, no matter where it led.

10

The Scholar in the Shadows

Luke blinked against the blinding light, his breath catching in his throat as the familiar, dizzying sensation of transportation washed over him. The world spun, twisted, and then suddenly, with a soft thud, he and Naomi landed on solid ground.

He stumbled forward, his sneakers scuffing the stone beneath his feet. The air was different—warmer, drier, and filled with the scent of sea salt and something earthy, ancient. Luke squinted, adjusting to the new brightness, and when his vision cleared, he gasped.

They were standing in the middle of a bustling city square, unlike anything they'd ever seen. People in flowing robes and tunics hurried past, some carrying scrolls, others pushing carts loaded with fruits and goods Luke couldn't even identify. Towering columns and grand buildings loomed on every side, their intricate carvings catching the sunlight that poured in from the brilliant blue sky above.

"This is... amazing," Naomi breathed, turning in a slow circle as she took in the ancient city around them.

Luke, standing beside her, looked around with wide eyes. "Where are we?" he muttered, his voice a mix of awe and confusion. "This doesn't look like any history class I've ever taken."

Naomi's heart raced as she pieced it together. The architecture, the clothes, the smell of parchment and ink that seemed to drift in the air—it all pointed to one place. "Alexandria," she whispered, her eyes lighting up. "We're in Alexandria."

"Wait," Luke said, frowning. "Like, ancient Alexandria? The place with the giant library and all that history stuff?"

Naomi nodded, excitement bubbling up inside her. "Yes! This is where scholars and scientists gathered from all over the world to study. This is the city where knowledge was everything."

Before Luke could respond, a loud clamor drew their attention. A group of men, carrying armfuls of scrolls, rushed past them, their faces tight with worry. A couple of soldiers, dressed in leather armor, followed behind, shouting orders in a language neither Naomi nor Luke could understand.

Naomi's eyes narrowed. Something was wrong. The hurried movements, the way people whispered and darted glances over their shoulders—it wasn't just a normal day in ancient Alexandria. Something was happening.

"Uh, Naomi," Luke said, his voice low. "I don't think we're here for a tour."

Naomi's pulse quickened, the weight of the glowing book in her backpack suddenly feeling heavier. She glanced around, trying to figure out where they were supposed to go, what they were supposed to do. But before she could make a move, a voice hissed from the shadows.

"You! Over here!"

Naomi and Luke turned, startled. Standing in the narrow alleyway between two stone buildings was a young woman, no older than sixteen. Her dark hair was tied back in a simple braid, and her eyes were sharp, darting between the soldiers and the two of them. She wore a plain tunic, and in her hands, she clutched a bundle of scrolls wrapped tightly in cloth.

"Come on!" she whispered urgently. "Before they see you!"

Naomi didn't need any more convincing. She grabbed Luke's arm and pulled him toward the alley, where the girl beckoned them closer. As soon as they were out of sight from the main street, the girl let out a shaky breath.

"You're not from here, are you?" the girl asked, eyeing their clothes with suspicion. "What are you doing in Alexandria?"

Naomi exchanged a glance with Luke, her heart racing. She wasn't sure how much to tell this stranger, but something about the girl seemed trustworthy, and Naomi could sense that they were in the right place.

"We're... looking for someone," she said cautiously. "Someone who's trying to protect something important."

The girl's eyes widened slightly, and she glanced at the scrolls in her hands. "Then you must be here for the manuscripts," she whispered, her voice urgent. "I'm Sophia, a scholar. I've been hiding these scrolls from the Roman officials—they're trying to destroy anything that has to do with Christianity."

Luke stiffened. "Destroy? Why?"

Sophia's face hardened. "The emperor fears anything that challenges his authority. Christianity is growing, and he wants to wipe out any trace of it. The library has already been raided once, and the soldiers are coming back to finish what they started."

Naomi's heart pounded. She could feel the gravity of the situation settling over her like a heavy cloak. "You're trying to save the manuscripts?"

Sophia nodded, her grip tightening on the bundle of scrolls. "Yes. These are biblical texts, some of the earliest copies. If they're destroyed, all of that knowledge will be lost forever."

Naomi felt a surge of determination rise within her. This was why they were here. To protect this knowledge—to preserve the light of faith and wisdom for future generations. She met Luke's eyes, seeing the same realization dawning in him.

"We'll help," Naomi said firmly. "Tell us what to do."

Sophia hesitated for a moment, studying them both, then nodded. "There's a hidden section of the library where some of the manuscripts are being kept. We need to move them to a safer place, but we have to be careful. The soldiers are everywhere."

Naomi's mind raced as she considered the task ahead. It wasn't just about sneaking through the streets—it was about outsmarting the soldiers, protecting the texts, and finding a way to keep this knowledge alive. Her love for history and science suddenly felt like a lifeline, a way to approach the problem with logic and creativity.

Luke, sensing the tension, stepped forward. "I'm good at thinking on my feet," he said, his tone more confident than Naomi had ever heard it. "Maybe we can create a distraction or something, give us enough time to move the scrolls."

Sophia raised an eyebrow but didn't dismiss the idea. "We'll need every advantage we can get," she said. "Follow me. But stay close—one wrong move, and we're all caught."

Naomi and Luke exchanged a quick glance, then fell in step behind Sophia as she led them deeper into the city. The narrow alleys twisted and turned, and the further they went, the more tense the atmosphere became. The sounds of soldiers marching grew louder in the distance, but Sophia seemed to know where to go, keeping them out of sight.

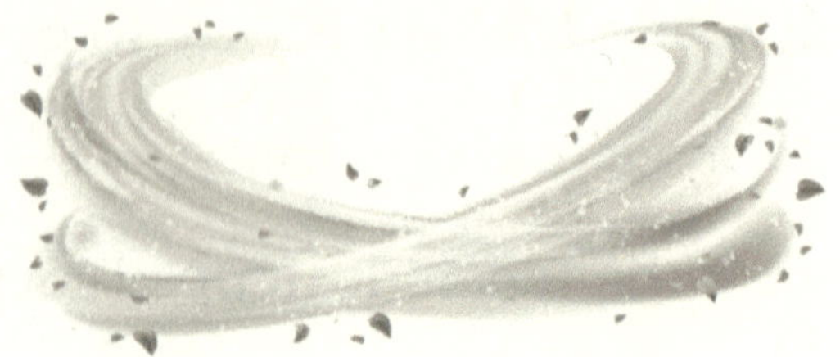

As they approached the library's back entrance, Naomi's heart raced. The massive structure loomed before them, its stone walls cold and imposing. The library of Alexandria—once a beacon of knowledge and wisdom—was now a battleground for the truth.

Sophia stopped just outside a small, unmarked door. "The manuscripts are inside," she whispered. "We'll need to move quickly."

Luke took a deep breath, steeling himself for what was to come. He glanced at Naomi, who gave him a small nod of encouragement. This was it. This was their mission.

"Let's protect the light," Naomi whispered.

And with that, they pushed open the door and stepped into the shadows of history, ready to preserve the flame of faith and knowledge for generations to come.

"This is one of the last safe places," Sophia explained as they entered the building. Inside, the air was cool and smelled of old parchment and ink. Scrolls and codices were stacked along the walls, their edges worn and fragile. "Here, we've gathered the most important manuscripts we could save. But we're running out of time."

Naomi's heart swelled with a mixture of awe and fear as she looked around the room. These were the texts that held centuries of knowledge, of faith, of history. And they were in danger of being lost forever.

"We need to move them," Naomi said, her voice firm. "Quickly."

Sophia nodded. "Yes, but we must be careful. The Romans are watching, and if they catch us…"

Luke stepped forward, his mind already racing with ideas. "What if we create a diversion? Something to throw them off while we move the manuscripts?"

Sophia glanced at him, intrigued. "What do you have in mind?"

Luke grinned, his eyes lighting up with excitement. "Leave it to me. I've got a plan."

Naomi watched as Luke's confidence grew, and for the first time since they arrived, she felt a surge of hope. They weren't just here to witness history—they were here to protect it.

And together, they were going to make sure the light of knowledge and faith didn't fade.

11

OUT OF TIME

THE COOL AIR INSIDE the library felt like a refuge from the scorching heat outside. Naomi's breath caught in her throat as her eyes adjusted to the dimly lit room. Scrolls and manuscripts lined the shelves, their ancient pages yellowed with age, and a distinct, musty scent filled the space. Each one of these fragile documents represented centuries of knowledge, faith, and history.

"We don't have much time," Sophia whispered, moving quickly along the shelves. Her hands were steady as she began gathering a bundle of manuscripts. "The Roman soldiers will be back soon."

Naomi's heart thudded in her chest as she followed Sophia. "Where will we move them?"

"There's an underground passage that leads to a safe house outside the city," Sophia replied, wrapping the manuscripts tightly in cloth to protect them. "But we need to get there without drawing attention."

Luke stood by the door, his eyes scanning the room as if expecting soldiers to burst through at any moment. "I'll go set the diversion," he said, glancing back at Naomi and Sophia. "Once it's in place, you two can move the manuscripts while I keep the guards distracted."

Naomi turned to him, her brow furrowed with concern. "Are you sure? It's risky, Luke."

Luke gave a small, confident grin, though there was a flicker of uncertainty in his eyes. "I've got this. Trust me."

Naomi nodded, her stomach tightening as she watched him slip out of the room. She wanted to believe that Luke could pull it off, but the weight of what they were trying to do pressed heavily on her. They were responsible for protecting these priceless texts, and if they failed, centuries of wisdom could be lost forever.

"Come on," Sophia said, snapping Naomi out of her thoughts. "We need to get these ready to move."

They worked quickly, gathering the manuscripts and securing them as best they could. Naomi's fingers trembled slightly as she held one of the scrolls, the fragile papyrus crinkling beneath her touch. It was hard to believe that she was holding something so ancient, so important. Her love for history had never felt more real, more urgent. But with every moment that passed, the threat of the soldiers loomed larger.

Suddenly, the distant clamor of voices reached them, muffled but growing louder. Naomi froze, her heart pounding in her ears.

"They're coming," she whispered, glancing at Sophia.

Sophia's face tightened. "We need to move now."

Naomi slung her bag over her shoulder, carefully placing the manuscripts inside. She and Sophia hurried toward the back entrance, the air around them thick with tension. Naomi's mind raced, praying that Luke's plan would work.

They reached the door just as the voices grew nearer. Sophia peeked outside, her eyes scanning the narrow alley that led away from the library. It was clear—for now.

"Let's go," Sophia said, leading the way.

Naomi followed closely, the weight of the manuscripts pressing against her back. Every sound felt magnified—the shuffle of their feet on the stone, the distant murmur of voices, the flutter of birds over-head. The narrow alleyways twisted and turned, and Naomi struggled to keep up with Sophia's swift movements. She couldn't help but think of Luke. Was he okay? Had he been caught?

Just as they rounded another corner, the sharp sound of a shout echoed through the alley. Naomi's blood ran cold. She turned, her heart hammering in her chest, and saw two Roman soldiers rushing toward them from the direction of the library.

"They've found us!" Naomi gasped.

Sophia's eyes widened with fear. "We have to run!"

They sprinted through the alley, the manuscripts bouncing against Naomi's back as her legs burned from the effort. She could hear the soldiers' heavy footsteps behind them, the clatter of their armor sending a surge of panic through her. They were getting closer.

As they raced around another corner, a figure suddenly stepped out of the shadows ahead of them. Naomi's heart leapt—Luke.

"Over here!" Luke called, motioning for them to follow. He was breathless, but his eyes were sharp with determination.

Without hesitation, Naomi and Sophia darted toward him, following him down a narrow side street that seemed to lead deeper into the city. The soldiers' shouts grew fainter behind them, but Naomi knew they weren't out of danger yet.

"Did it work?" Naomi asked breathlessly as they ran.

Luke gave a quick nod, his voice tight with exhaustion. "I set a fire in the market. It's small, but it should keep the guards busy for a while."

Naomi's heart swelled with relief, though the tension in her body remained. Luke's plan had bought them some time, but they still had to reach the underground passage. They couldn't stop now.

They continued weaving through the city's winding streets, the distant sounds of chaos in the market keeping the soldiers distracted for the moment. But Naomi could feel the urgency building inside her. If they were caught, everything would be lost.

Finally, they reached the entrance to the underground passage. It was hidden behind a crumbling stone wall, barely noticeable except for a small, rusted door tucked away in the shadows.

"This way," Sophia said, pushing the door open.

They stepped inside, the air immediately cooler and damp with the scent of earth. The narrow passage stretched ahead of them, dimly lit by torches mounted on the walls. Naomi could hear the faint drip of water echoing in the distance, and the soft shuffle of their feet on the stone floor was the only other sound that broke the stillness.

For the first time since they'd begun their mission, Naomi felt a sliver of hope. They were almost there. The manuscripts were safe for now.

As they moved deeper into the passage, Luke walked beside Naomi, his breath still coming in shallow gasps. "We did it," he whispered, a hint of disbelief in his voice.

Naomi nodded, her own relief bubbling up inside her. "You were amazing," she said, her voice low but filled with admiration. "I don't know how you thought of that plan so quickly."

Luke gave a small, tired smile. "I just... did what I could. But we still have to make sure these manuscripts stay hidden."

They continued walking, the passage gradually widening into a larger chamber. At the far end of the room, a series of stone shelves lined the walls, ready to hold the manuscripts they'd saved.

Sophia stepped forward, her face softening with relief. "We can leave them here. This place is hidden well enough that the soldiers won't find it. For now, the manuscripts are safe."

Naomi and Luke exchanged a glance, their hearts pounding with the realization of what they'd accomplished. Together, they had protected centuries of knowledge—of faith and history—and ensured that the light of wisdom wouldn't be extinguished.

But even as the relief washed over them, Naomi couldn't shake the feeling that their journey was far from over. The glowing book in her backpack seemed to pulse gently, as if reminding her that there were still more missions to complete, more light to protect.

Naomi took a deep breath, her hand brushing against the warm cover of the book. They had made it this far. Whatever came next, they would face it together.

12

The Flame Preserved

Naomi sat on the cold stone floor of the underground chamber, the soft glow of the torches casting flickering shadows on the walls. The manuscripts lay safely on the shelves, their fragile pages protected, at least for now. A heavy silence filled the room, broken only by the faint dripping of water echoing through the passageways.

Luke leaned against the wall, his chest still rising and falling with the effort of their escape. He stared at the floor, his brow furrowed, the weight of what they had just done starting to sink in.

Sophia stood near the entrance, her eyes scanning the room as if waiting for something—perhaps for the tension to lift, or for the realization that they were truly safe. Her hands still clutched one last manuscript, and she handled it with the utmost care, as though holding a delicate flame that could be extinguished at any moment.

"We did it," Naomi whispered, her voice barely audible in the stillness. "We actually did it."

Luke gave a tired smile, but there was a flicker of uncertainty in his eyes. "Yeah, but for how long? The Romans will keep coming. What if they find this place?"

Sophia stepped forward, her face calm but serious. "That's always the risk. But what you both did today—it gave us more time. It allowed us to preserve these texts for a little longer. And sometimes, that's all we can hope for."

Naomi felt a knot tighten in her stomach. She knew Sophia was right. They had saved the manuscripts, but the fight to protect knowledge and faith wasn't over. It was never really over. There would always be forces trying to snuff out the light of truth. But as long as people like Sophia, and even people like Luke and herself, kept fighting, the light would survive.

Naomi glanced at the glowing book in her back-pack, its warmth pressing against her spine as if reminding her that their mission was far from complete. She could feel its gentle pulse, as though it were alive, waiting for them to take the next step.

"What happens now?" Luke asked, his voice soft but steady.

Sophia placed the last manuscript carefully on the shelf and turned to face them. "Now, we do what we've always done. We keep learning. We keep fighting. The light of knowledge and faith must be protected, and as long as we have breath, we will protect it."

Naomi's chest tightened with a mixture of admiration and fear. How could someone like Sophia, living in constant danger, carry such a burden? How could she keep fighting when the darkness seemed so overwhelming? Naomi thought of Joan of Arc, of the courage it took to step into battle knowing the odds were against you. And now, here was Sophia, standing in the same fight centuries earlier.

Luke's gaze shifted to Naomi, his expression thoughtful. "Do you think... we'll have to keep doing this?" he asked, his voice barely above a whisper. "I mean, what if the book takes us somewhere even more dangerous?"

Naomi met his eyes, and for a moment, she didn't know how to answer. She had felt the same fear—wondered the same thing. But something inside her, something that had been growing since their first adventure, pushed her forward. She thought of Joan's faith, Sophia's determination, and the countless people who had carried the light before them.

"I don't know," she admitted. "But I think we're here for a reason. We can't just... walk away."

Luke stared at her for a moment, his face a mixture of apprehension and quiet resolve. "Yeah. I guess you're right."

Before Naomi could say anything more, the book in her backpack pulsed again, its warmth suddenly intensifying. The sensation sent a shiver down her spine, and she could feel its call, tugging at her, drawing her toward it. Luke noticed her stiffen, his eyes widening as he stepped closer.

"What is it?" he asked, glancing at her bag.

Naomi slowly pulled the book out of her backpack, its cover glowing with a soft, golden light. The ancient pages flickered to life, and once again, the strange symbols began shifting and transforming into words they could understand. Luke leaned over, reading the message as it appeared.

"The light has been protected, but the journey continues. New paths await. The bearers must remain steadfast, for the darkness will not rest."

Naomi's breath caught in her throat. The message was clear: their mission wasn't over.

Luke exhaled sharply, running a hand through his hair. "So... we're not done?"

Naomi shook her head, her heart racing. "No. The book is telling us there's more we have to do."

Sophia watched them quietly, her expression un-readable. "Wherever the light takes you," she said softly, "remember that you're never alone. There will always be others, fighting to keep the flame alive. You are part of something much bigger than yourselves."

Naomi swallowed hard, her gaze drifting to the glowing pages of the book. She could feel the weight of Sophia's words, the responsibility that came with carrying the light. It wasn't just about them—it was about everyone who had come before and everyone who would come after. They were part of a legacy, a mission that spanned time and space.

Luke took a deep breath, his hands resting on his knees. "I guess that means we should get ready."

Naomi nodded, feeling a surge of determination rising within her. She glanced at Sophia, her voice steady. "We'll do our part. We'll keep fighting."

Sophia gave a small, approving smile. "I believe you will."

Just then, the room seemed to blur around them, the edges of the chamber dissolving into a swirl of golden light. Naomi felt the familiar sensation of weightlessness as the world began to shift. She reached out instinctively, grabbing Luke's hand as the light enveloped them.

Sophia's figure faded from view, but her voice lingered, echoing in the distance. "The light will guide you. Trust in it."

The swirling light grew brighter, pulling them into its embrace. Naomi's heart pounded as the world around them disappeared, replaced by the endless expanse of light. It felt like being suspended between moments, between worlds—an infinite space where time no longer mattered.

The air was cooler now, tinged with the scent of damp earth and fresh grass. Naomi blinked, her eyes adjusting to the dim light filtering through the broken windows of a familiar place. Her heart skipped a beat as the haze of light around them faded completely, revealing their surroundings.

They were back.

Luke, who had been standing beside her, froze mid-step. His brow furrowed, and he glanced around the small, run-down chapel. The same worn stone walls and crumbling altar stood before them. The place where this whole adventure had begun—the old, abandoned church deep in the woods.

"We're home," Luke said, his voice barely above a whisper. There was a mixture of relief and confusion in his tone, as though he couldn't quite believe they were really back.

Naomi took a step forward, her sneakers scuffing against the dusty floor, sending small clouds of dirt into the air. She felt a chill run down her spine, but not from fear—rather, from the realization that everything had come full circle. The Chronicles of Light had brought them here, and now, it had brought them back.

Her fingers tightened around the glowing book, still warm in her hands. The familiar pulse was there, but it was quieter now, as if the book was settling, waiting for whatever came next. The faint golden light that had surrounded them moments before slowly dimmed, leaving the old chapel in shadows once again.

Luke exhaled, running a hand through his hair. "So...what happens now? Is it over?" His eyes darted toward the empty altar where they had first found the book, as though expecting something more to happen.

Naomi shook her head, though the certainty she had felt earlier was slipping. "I don't think it's over," she said softly. "But maybe...maybe it's a pause. The book brought us here for a reason, and I think it'll call us again when the time is right."

Luke frowned, clearly not satisfied with the answer, but he nodded. "Yeah, I guess that makes sense. This whole thing has been…" He trailed off, struggling to find the right words. "Weird. But kind of amazing too."

Naomi smiled slightly, though her mind was still racing with everything they had experienced. The ancient manuscripts, Joan of Arc's courage, the battles they'd fought to protect the light of faith and knowledge—it all felt like a dream. But the weight of the book in her hands reminded her that it was very real.

"I think we've been chosen for something bigger than we realize," Naomi said, her voice thoughtful. "It's like what Sophia said—there are others, all over the world, all throughout time, fighting to keep the light alive. And we're a part of that now."

Luke glanced at her, his expression softening. "I guess you're right. We've been through a lot, huh?"

Naomi nodded, the memories of their journey flashing through her mind. She didn't know what the future held or when the book would call them again, but one thing was clear—whatever came next, they were ready for it.

The silence of the old chapel settled around them, heavy and peaceful. The sun outside was beginning to set, casting long shadows across the stone floor. Naomi took a deep breath, her heart finally slowing after the whirlwind of their latest adventure.

"I think we should get back home," Luke said, breaking the quiet. He glanced out one of the broken windows, where the orange glow of the setting sun filtered through the trees. "Our families are probably wondering where we've been."

Naomi chuckled, a bit of the tension easing from her shoulders. "Yeah, you're right. We've been gone a lot longer than they think."

As they turned toward the door, Naomi cast one last glance at the glowing book in her hands. It was quiet now, the light dimmed but not extinguished.

She tucked it carefully into her backpack, feeling its comforting warmth against her back. It wasn't finished with them yet—she could feel it. The light would call them again.

Together, they stepped outside, leaving the forgotten chapel behind. The woods around them were quiet, the air cool and fresh. Naomi breathed it in, the familiar scent of pine and damp earth grounding her after everything they had been through.

"We'll be ready," Luke said, his voice confident as they made their way through the woods. "Next time the book needs us, we'll be ready."

Naomi smiled, her heart lighter now. "Yeah, we will."

As they walked, the sun dipped lower on the horizon, painting the sky in hues of pink and gold. The light was fading, but it wasn't gone. And neither was their journey.

They'd return to school, to their normal lives, but they would carry with them the knowledge that they had been chosen to protect something far greater. The Chronicles of Light had brought them back to where it all began, but Naomi knew, deep down, that this was just the beginning.

And whatever came next, they would protect the light—together.

As the last rays of sunlight slipped behind the trees, the air filled with the quiet promise of new adventures waiting to be written.

To be continued...

Biblical Reflections

Messages from the Chronicle of Light

In *Lost Chronicles of Light,* Naomi and Luke's adventures are more than just thrilling time-travel escapades; they are filled with messages that speak to the heart of faith, courage, and divine guidance. Each message revealed in the *Chronicle of Light* as they journey through pivotal moments in history is deeply connected to Scripture, grounding their experiences in timeless biblical truths. These passages highlight the ongoing battle between light and darkness, the vital importance of steadfast faith, and the perseverance required to face trials with courage.

This chapter provides the Scripture references that echo the messages found within the *Chronicle of Light.* By exploring these verses, readers can gain a deeper appreciation of how each lesson Naomi and Luke encounter is a reflection of God's eternal wisdom. These passages not only illuminate the characters' paths but also offer insight into our own lives, reminding us that the light of God's truth is always there to guide, protect, and inspire.

As you read through these verses, take a moment to reflect on how they resonate with the unfolding story. They serve as spiritual anchors, connecting the adventures of Naomi and Luke to the greater narrative of God's unchanging love and light. Let these scriptures deepen your understanding of the journey and remind you that, no matter the darkness faced, the light of faith will always prevail.

"The world's light fades, but not all is lost. The bearers must travel through time, through space, to protect the light from darkness... They are chosen to walk with the heroes of faith, to guard the light of hope."

1. "The world's light fades, but not all is lost."

Scripture Reference: John 1:5 (NIV): *"The light shines in the darkness, and the darkness has not overcome it."*

This verse reassures that even when the world's light seems to fade, the light of Christ still shines and will never be overcome by darkness.

2. "The bearers must travel through time, through space, to protect the light from darkness."

Scripture Reference: Ephesians 6:12 (NIV):

"For our struggle is not against flesh and blood, but against the rulers, against the authorities, against the powers of this dark world and against the spiritual forces of evil in the heavenly realms."

This verse emphasizes the spiritual battle between light and darkness, suggesting that those called to protect the light must face both physical and spiritual challenges that transcend time and space.

3. **"They are chosen to walk with the heroes of faith..."**

Scripture Reference: Hebrews 12:1 (NIV):

"Therefore, since we are surrounded by such a great cloud of witnesses, let us throw off everything that hinders and the sin that so easily entangles. And let us run with perseverance the race marked out for us."

This passage reminds us that believers are part of a spiritual legacy, walking in the footsteps of the heroes of faith who came before, such as those mentioned in Hebrews 11.

4. "…to guard the light of hope."

Scripture Reference: 1 Peter 3:15 (NIV): *"But in your hearts revere Christ as Lord. Always be prepared to give an answer to everyone who asks you to give the reason for the hope that you have. But do this with gentleness and   respect."*

This verse encourages believers to protect and defend the light of hope, sharing it with others while guarding it within themselves.

"The light must not fade. Protect the flame of faith. The sanctuary must remain hidden. The

way forward is through faith, not battle. Trust in the light. It will guide you."

1. "The light must not fade."

Scripture Reference: Matthew 5:14-16 (NIV): "You are the light of the world. A town built on a hill cannot be hidden. Neither do people light a lamp and put it under a bowl. Instead, they put it on its stand, and it gives light to everyone in the house. In the same way, let your light shine before others, that they may see your good deeds and glorify your Father in heaven."

This verse speaks to the responsibility of believers to let their light shine and not allow it to fade.

2. "Protect the flame of faith."

Scripture Reference: 2 Timothy 1:14 (NIV): "Guard the good deposit that was entrusted to you—guard it with the help of the Holy Spirit who lives in us."

This passage reflects the need to protect the faith we have been given, just as the flame of faith must be guarded and nurtured.

3. "The sanctuary must remain hidden."

Scripture Reference: Psalm 27:5 (NIV): "For in the day of trouble He will keep me safe in His dwelling; He will hide me in the shelter of His sacred tent and set me high upon a rock."

This verse speaks of God hiding His people in times of trouble, much like a hidden sanctuary that provides protection and safety.

4. "The way forward is through faith, not battle."

Scripture Reference: Zechariah 4:6 (NIV): "So he said to me, 'This is the word of the Lord to Zerubbabel: Not by might nor by power, but by My Spirit,' says the Lord Almighty."

This passage emphasizes that true victory and progress come through faith in God's Spirit, not through physical battle or strength.

5. "Trust in the light. It will guide you."

Scripture Reference: Psalm 119:105 (NIV): "Your word is a lamp for my feet, a light on my path."

This verse reflects the idea of trusting in the light—God's word and presence—to guide us through life.

"The light must not fade. Protect the flame of faith. You are the bearers of the light, chosen to shield it from the darkness."

1. "The light must not fade."

Scripture Reference: Matthew 5:14-16 (NIV):

"You are the light of the world. A town built on a hill cannot be hidden. Neither do people light a lamp and put it under a bowl. Instead, they put it on its stand, and it gives light to everyone in the house. In the same way, let your light shine before others, that they may see your good deeds and glorify your Father in heaven."

This passage highlights the importance of letting our light—our faith and good works—shine for the world to see, ensuring that it doesn't fade.

2. "Protect the flame of faith."

Scripture Reference: 2 Timothy 1:13-14 (NIV):

"What you heard from me, keep as the pattern of sound teaching, with faith and love in Christ Jesus. Guard the good deposit that was entrusted to you—guard it with the help of the Holy Spirit who lives in us."

This verse encourages believers to protect and guard the faith that has been entrusted to them, much like protecting a flame from being extinguished.

3. "You are the bearers of the light, chosen to shield it from the darkness."

Scripture Reference: Ephesians 5:8-9 (NIV): "For you were once darkness, but now you are light in the Lord. Live as children of light (for the fruit of the light consists in all goodness, righteousness, and truth)."

This passage reflects the idea that believers are chosen to be bearers of light, called to live in righteousness and goodness, actively shielding that light from the darkness of sin and evil.

"The light will guide you through the darkness, but you must have the courage to follow it."

    1. "The light will guide you through the dar kness..."

Scripture Reference: John 8:12 (NIV): "When Jesus spoke again to the people, He said, 'I am the light of the world. Whoever follows me will never walk in darkness, but will have the light of life.'"

This verse emphasizes that Jesus is the light guiding us through the darkness, offering life and direction for those who follow Him.

    2. "...but you must have the courage..."

Scripture Reference: Joshua 1:9 (NIV): "Have I not commanded you? Be strong and courageous. Do not be afraid; do not be discouraged, for the Lord your God will be with you wherever you go."

This verse encourages believers to be strong and courageous, trusting that God is with them in every challenge they face.

3. "...to follow it."

Scripture Reference: Psalm 119:105 (NIV): "Your word is a lamp for my feet, a light on my path."

This verse reflects the importance of following God's guidance, as His word is the light that leads us in the right direction.

"The time has come for a new bearer. The light seeks those who doubt, those who fear, and those who are called to believe. Step forward in faith, and the path will be revealed."

1. "The time has come for a new bearer."

Scripture Reference: Isaiah 6:8 (NIV): "Then I heard the voice of the Lord saying, 'Whom shall I send? And who will go for us?' And I said, 'Here am I. Send me!'"

This verse speaks of being called to take up a mission or responsibility, just as the message refers to the time for a new bearer.

2. "The light seeks those who doubt..."

Scripture Reference: Jude 1:22 (NIV): "Be merciful to those who doubt."

This passage reflects the idea that God understands and reaches out to those who struggle with doubt.

3. "...those who fear..."

Scripture Reference: Isaiah 41:10 (NIV): "So do not fear, for I am with you; do not be dismayed, for I am your God. I will strengthen you and help you; I will uphold you with my righteous right hand."

This verse reassures those who are afraid that God is with them, providing strength and support.

4. "...and those who are called to believe."

Scripture Reference: John 6:29 (NIV): "Jesus answered, 'The work of God is this: to believe in the one he has sent.'"

This verse emphasizes the importance of belief and faith in following God's call.

5. "Step forward in faith, and the path will be revealed."

Scripture Reference: 2 Corinthians 5:7 (NIV): "For we live by faith, not by sight."

This passage reflects the idea of stepping forward in faith, trusting that God will reveal the path ahead, even when it is not immediately visible.

"The light has been protected, but the journey continues. New paths await. The bearers must remain steadfast, for the darkness will not rest."

1. **"The light has been protected, but the journey continues."**

Scripture Reference: John 8:12 (NIV): "When Jesus spoke again to the people, he said, 'I am the light of the world. Whoever follows me will never walk in darkness, but will have the light of life.'"

This verse speaks to the protection and continuation of the light through faith in Christ.

2. **"New paths await."**

Scripture Reference: Isaiah 43:19 (NIV): "See, I am doing a new thing! Now it springs up; do you not perceive it? I am making a way in the wilderness and streams in the wasteland."

God often leads us on new paths and guides us into new journeys, even when we don't expect them.

3. **"The bearers must remain steadfast."**

Scripture Reference: 1 Corinthians 15:58 (NIV): "Therefore, my dear brothers and sisters, stand firm. Let nothing move you. Always give yourselves fully to the work of the Lord, because you know that your labor in the Lord is not in vain."

This verse encourages steadfastness and faithfulness in carrying out God's work.

4. "For the darkness will not rest."

Scripture Reference: Ephesians 6:12 (NIV): "For our struggle is not against flesh and blood, but against the rulers, against the authorities, against the powers of this dark world and against the spiritual forces of evil in the heavenly realms."

This verse reminds us that darkness is always present, and believers must remain vigilant in their spiritual battle.

About the Author

Abbie Rose

Abbie Rose is a Bestselling Amazon romance author known for weaving tales of passion, heartache, and ultimate triumph in the world of love. With a gift for creating unforgettable char-acters and immersive stories, Abbie's novels have captured the hearts of readers around the globe, earning her a loyal following.

Born with a love for storytelling, Abbie began her writing journey at a young age, filling notebooks with tales of romance and adventure. When she's not writing, Abbie enjoys traveling, indulging in classic romance novels, and exploring the latest trends in marketing and storytelling. She lives with her family in the Houston-Metro, where she continues to dream up new stories that inspire, entertain, and remind us all of the power of love.

Also by Abbie Rose

Sweet & Clean Romance

Ace's Heart: An Ex-Mafia, 2ndChance, Christian Romance

Devotionals & Motivational

Blessed Nourishment Vol. 1 (paperback only)

49 Days of Self-Discovery

Prince, Not Required: Slaying your inner dragons, without dropping your crown!

Business

Boss Babe Publishing: The Ultimate Self-Publishing Guide and Workbook

The Carter Effect: Hip-Hop 101

Boss Babe by Design

Children's Books

Did you know that I also wrote children's books under the pen name, Abbie Rose? In my books hang out with me, as I teach Duke his puppy manners. These books teach young children the importance of taking care of and training their dogs. Helping them to develop a trusting and safe relationship with their dog, under a parent's guidance, and in a fun way.

Welcome Home Duke

Duke Learns His Name

Duke Learns Sit